This facsimile of Margaret Bruce's 1965 publication has been issued by Wishan Books, with special thanks to Clive Harper and the Herts Folklore Research Society.

Please note that Margaret Bruce died over twenty years ago so there is no point in contacting her at the Yarm Road address. You will not get a reply.

WISHAN
BOOKS
2022

Wishan Books is an independent publishing house dedicated to making facsimile editions of publications significant to the history of the Wica available to modern researchers.

THE LITTLE GRIMOIRE

by

Margaret Bruce

By the same author:

A LITTLE TREASURY OF LOVE & MAGICK

PREFACE

In the days when country doctors were as scarce as hens' teeth, every village Wise Woman who could read and write kept a Grimoire, a hand written book of recipes and spells. When that most dangerous and pathetic of delusions, the witch-mania, was at its height, most of these Grimoires were destroyed or lost in the reign of terror and madness. This book is an attempt to re-create, with the help of a little artistic licence, such a Grimoire. If you find a jam or wine recipe among the spells, it is because the Wise Woman, who lived so very close to Birth, Death and the Forces of Nature, did not divide human experience into convenient categories like "natural" and "supernatural". Her simple and unsophisticated attitude to life enabled her to see the very real Magick that went into the creation of a loaf of bread or a cask of good Ale.

On the other hand, age alone lends no virtue to false ideas. It is as well therefore to bear in mind that in every Grimoire, you will find, for each pinch of ancient wisdom, a whole peck of ancient folly.

Grimoires were usually handed down from generation to generation, each owner adding her own favourite snippets of knowledge. A really fine example might contain, in addition to Herbal Lore and Spells, a collection of cookery recipes, gardening hints and household wrinkles. Between the leaves one might find pressed herbs, a lock of hair or a fragment of material from a favourite dress. In short, the Grimoire was not just a recipe book but a personal treasure.

Margaret Bruce.

1

Miss Margaret Bruce

Prayer To The Earth Mother

Take a handful of fine Earth and sprinkle it in a circle about thee saying in a clear voice:-

ERCE, ERCE, ERCE,
MOTHER OF EARTH,
HAIL TO THEE EARTH,
MOTHER OF MEN!
BE FRUITFUL
IN GOD'S EMBRACE;
FILLED WITH FOOD
FOR THE USE OF MEN.

Then take every kind of meal and have a small loaf baked no bigger than the palm of thy hand, having kneaded it with milk and Spring Water, and lay it under the first turned furrow.

The Planetary

Planet	Angel	Metal	Stone	Incense
☉	Michael	Gold	Amber	Mastic
☽	Gabriel	Silver	Selenite	Myrtle
♂	Samael	Iron	Hæmatite	Lig. Aloes
☿	Raphael	Mercury	Lodestone	Cinnamon
♃	Sachiel	Tin	Carnelian	Nutmeg
♀	Anael	Copper	Coral	Saffron
♄	Cassiel	Lead	Jet	Pepperwort

Correspondences

Colour	Perfume	Herb	Sigil
Orange	Neroli	Juniper	
White	Nicotiana	Poppy	
Red	Civet	Urtica	
Yellow	Lavender	Coriander	
Blue	Ambergris	Cedar	
Green	Stephanotis	Verbena	
Black	Violet	Hellebore	

The Moon

ecause she doth wondrously affect the lives of men and beasts and doth aid or hinder divers works; therefore be dilligent in thy observance of her movements.

Sowing and planting may best be done as the Moon waxeth, for all things thus begun must needs prosper. If thou wouldst banish rats from thy barn, poverty from thy house, or an enemy from thy gates; begin thy operation when the Moon waneth that thy purpose may the better be fulfilled.

Observe also that when Luna occupies a Water sign, then works of destruction may be accomplished. The Crab, the Scorpion and the Fishes are of this element. In the signs of the Ram, the Archer and the Lion, she is powerful for Love. The Bull, the Virgin, and the Goat give treasures when Luna dwells thus. Of the air, these signs govern doubtful sciences and all strange experiments. The Scales, the Twins and the Water-bearer are of this realm.

THE FOUR WITCHES. (Dürer.)

7

A Prayer To The Sun

Turn towards the East and, bowing humbly nine times, say the following words:—

"EASTWARDS I STAND, FOR FAVOURS I PRAY.
I PRAY THE GREAT LORD, I PRAY THE MIGHTY PRINCE.
I PRAY THE HOLY WARDEN OF THE HEAVENLY KINGDOM.
TO EARTH I PRAY AND TO UP-HEAVEN . . ."

Then turn three times sunwise, prostrate thyself upon the ground and say the Litany . . .

Some Zodiacal Perfumes

ARIES.	Civet, Patchouli or Magnolia.
TAURUS.	Stephanotis, Verbena or Lotus.
GEMINI.	Tuberose, Lavender or Fennel.
CANCER.	Night-scented Stock or Jasmine.
LEO.	Neroli, Heliotrope or Bergamot.
VIRGO.	Lavender, Tuberose or Fougere.
LIBRA.	Stephanotis, Vetivert or Musk.
SCORPIO.	Civet, Opoponax or Castoreum.
SAGITTARIUS.	Cedar, Russian Leather or Rose.
CAPRICORN.	Spikenard, Cassia or Pine.
AQUARIUS.	Wood Violet, Calamus or Clove.
PISCES.	Rose, Cedar or Palmarosa.

Some Zodiacal Correspondences

In primitive medicine, great attention was paid to the planetary and zodiacal rulings of the parts of the human body.

Although the jargon of astrology is used, the method was really a mnemonic system in which the whole of Creation was divided into seven basic groups of phenomena.

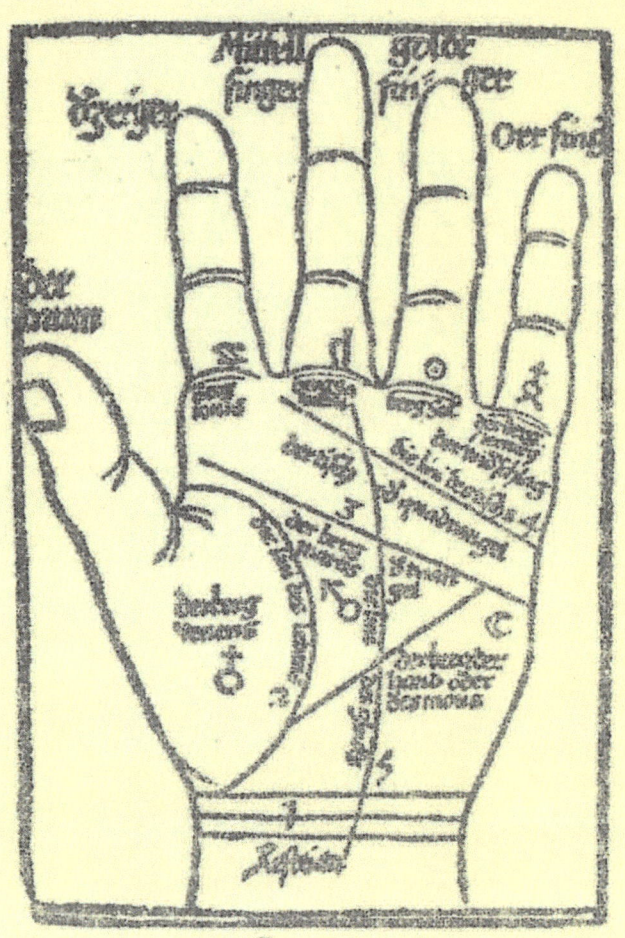

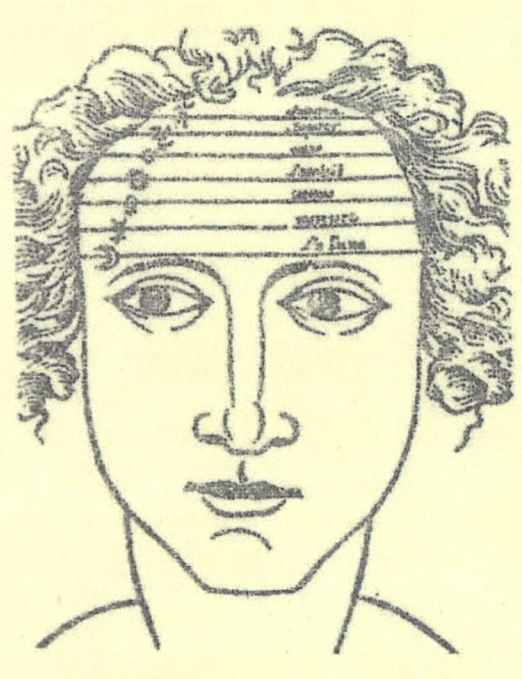

The allocation of anatomical areas to each sign of the Zodiac enabled the physician to select a remedy from amongst those herbs ruled by a planet sympathetic to the organ and opposed to the ailment.

10

The Powers Of The Planets

e who would command spirits must observe that each planet governs divers operations. Luna hath a peculiar influence on the tides and all bodily humours. She giveth silver and causeth movement of fishes and vessels. Her beams rule the courses of women and she may blight crops or bring abundance, according to her phase and aspect.

Sol giveth gold and honours and obtaineth favour in the sight of men.

Mars causeth wars and giveth great armies, many cannon and all manner of weapons. Brimstone and thunder are in his breath; also machines of destruction are under his dominion.

Mercury, the Great Hermes, the very Lord of Alchymy, doth rule words, books, and secrets of past present and future. He who invoketh in the Hour of Mercury may cast down the rich or raise the poor. By his wit shall he discover the secrets of hidden arts and sciences and open every lock and bolt, no matter how secure.

aturn ruleth all slow moving creatures that love darkness and hidden places. His spirit dwelleth in caves, tombs, prisons, mines, old buildings and ruins. He is the Lord of Time and moveth with leaden step, hindering those who would progress, yet fixing that which is volatile and unstable. By his hand are men slain and turned to stone. Still may he discover rich treasures and precious metals who seeketh dilligently when Saturn be well aspected.

Jupiter healeth distempers and obtaineth the favour of Judges, Princes, and those in high authority. He ruleth merriement and laughter and scorneth poverty. In his hour one may earn worldly success but he is accustomed to genteel company and smileth not on him who approacheth with tattered garment and fearful eye.

Venus be the Queen of Love and ruleth indolence and luxury in her hour. By her influence betrothals may prosper and the hearts of men burn with love and desire. She is fair of face and attire. She doth wear sweet ointments and speaketh with the voice of the dove. Who calls on her may obtain works of art, precious jewels and merry conceits of every sort.

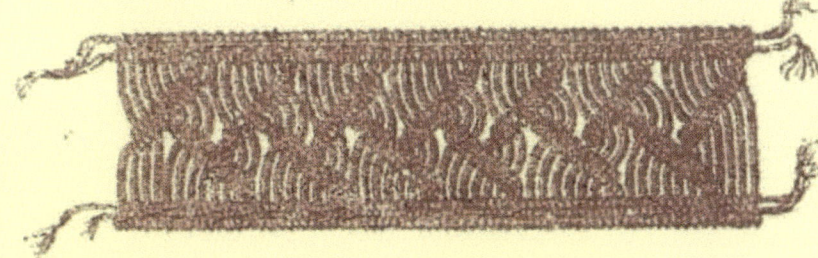

Some Zodiacal Suffumigations

ARIES.   Myrrh mixed with Yellow Sandalwood.

TAURUS. Frankincense mixed with Verbena.

GEMINI. Cinnamon mixed with Lavender.

CANCER. Myrtle mixed with Camphor Oil.

LEO.   Olibanum mixed with Juniper Berries.

VIRGO. Cinnamon mixed with Frankincense.

LIBRA. Saffron mixed with Frankincense.

SCORPIO. Opoponax mixed with Myrrh.

SAGITTARIUS. Myrrh mixed with Nutmeg.

CAPRICORN. Benzoin mixed with Myrrh.

AQUARIUS. Benzoin mixed with Violet Leaves.

PISCES. Nutmeg mixed with Frankincense.

ccult Alphabets are just another means of recording ideas prior to transforming them into concrete reality.

According to the "ethics" of bogus occultism it is desirable to have "powers" but wrong to use them for practical purposes. This is the philosophy of the charlatan and the self-deluded, for without the ultimate reality all is deception.

Writing and symbols are actually links between the amorphous realm of potentialities and the "real" world of physical being. Once an idea has been expressed in word or symbol it is on the way to becoming solid reality.

So-called spiritual exercises that stop short of this ultimate reality are not only a waste of time but a very real danger to mental health. Instead of precipitating ideas into the world of here-and-now reality, they leave the exploring mind stranded in a limbo of delusion.

Real Magick never loses touch with reality, regardless of the heights to which the imagination may soar in search of inspiration.

Whether you express your aims in Hebrew, Theban or plain English - remember; So let it be written. SO LET IT BE DONE!

HEBREW		"Alphabet of the Magi."		"Celestial" Writing		"Malachim"		"Passing the River"	
א	ן								
ב	ס								
ג	ע								
ד	פ								
ה	צ								
ו	ק								
ז	ר								
ח	ש								
ט	ת								
י									
כ									
ל									
מ									

16

Roman Equivalent of the foregoing scripts		"Theban" or "Honorian"		Roman Equivalent		Runic		Roman Equivalent	
A	N	(symbol)	(symbol)	A	N	(rune)	(rune)	f	t
B	S	(symbol)	(symbol)	B	O	(rune)	(rune)	u	b
G	O	(symbol)	(symbol)	C	P	(rune)	(rune)	th	e
D	P	(symbol)	(symbol)	D	Q	(rune)	(rune)	o	m
H	Tz	(symbol)	(symbol)	E	R	(rune)	(rune)	r	l
V	Q	(symbol)	(symbol)	F	S	(rune)	(rune)	k	ng
Z	R	(symbol)	(symbol)	G	T	(rune)	(rune)	g	oe
Ch	Sh	(symbol)	(symbol)	H	U	(rune)	(rune)	w	d
T	Th	(symbol)	(symbol)	I	V	(rune)	(rune)	h	a
I		(symbol)	(symbol)	J	W	(rune)	(rune)	n	ae
K		(symbol)	(symbol)	K	X	(rune)	(rune)	i	y
L		(symbol)	(symbol)	L	Y	(rune)	(rune)	gh	ea / c
M		(symbol)	(symbol)	M	Z	(rune)	(rune)	s	k / g

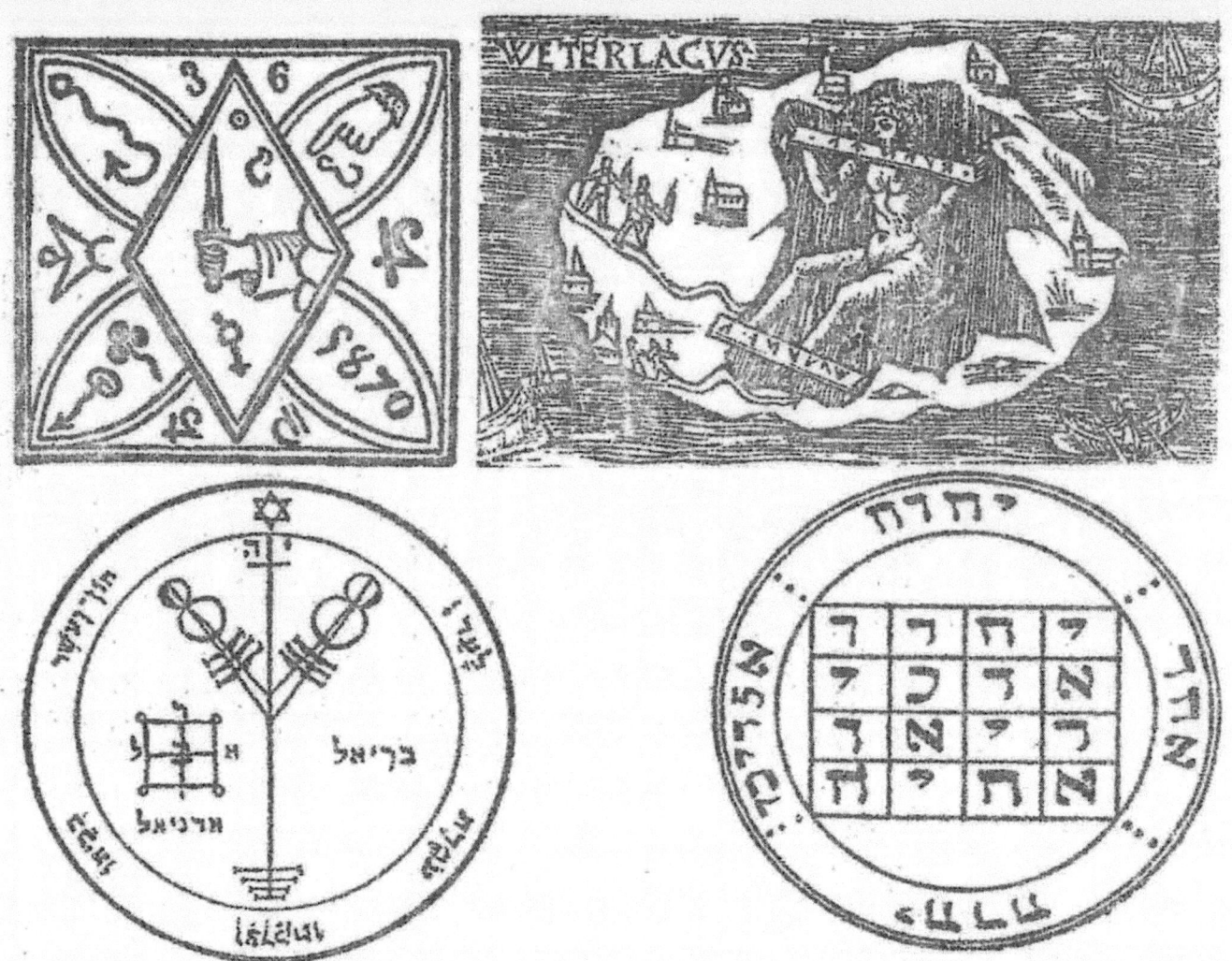

These talismans are the dead symbols of long
forgotten intentions. They are the used 'bus
tickets and obsolete currency notes of occultism and, as such, their contemporary signific-
ance is nil.

Effective modern talismans are notes
scribbled on a desk pad or preliminary sketches
on scraps of paper. When they have served their
purpose they are tossed into the waste basket.

Had waste baskets only been in vogue when
Solomon and Sheba were swapping status symbols
we might have been spared the cartloads of
esoteric garbage salvaged by occult scavengers
for the purpose of misleading and fleecing
the trusting "seeker after truth."

WISHAN WANDS.

The MAGICK WANDS OF THE WISHANS are a simple and unique method of assisting to integrate a human personality.

They can be used in conjunction with any religion or philosophy.

The MAGICK WANDS OF THE WISHANS will assist in the development of clairvoyant faculty.

Our Instructions and Chart are so arranged that they may be used for simple divination, or through various stages for more advanced results.

The system is not fortune-telling, but based on sound psychological principles.

NOTHING TO LEARN. YOU CAN GET THE ANSWER IN TEN SECONDS. SET OF SIX WANDS. WITH FULL INSTRUCTIONS FOR USE, & CHART. WITH RAINBOW JEWELLED ENDS........£1. 0. 0, post free U.K.

OBTAINABLE ONLY FROM

REG Dumblecott Magick Productions. Charlwood, Horley, Surrey.

Profits for the finding of the Water City.

Everybody knows that beauty is only skin deep.
Nevertheless, the Wise Woman - if she was
genuinely wise - knew that one of the most
effective bits of Magick is to make oneself as
attractive and appealing as possible.

Politicians and P.R.O.'s are beginning to
catch on to the idea but it is doubtful if they
will ever use the desperate and way-out methods
of improving the image that one is likely to
encounter in the pages of a grimoire.

To Hinder The Brests From Augmenting

Galen saith that if you use the juice of Ladies Mantle from the leaves of it, and wet linen in it, and lay it on the Brests, and renew it; it will not only delay Virgins' Brests from increasing, but will fasten the loose Brests of Matrons and mayke them firm.

Another Secret

To make the hands as white as Milk, bruise Almonds, Melon Seeds, Coucumber Seeds, and Crums of Bread; then make cakes of them with Barley Water wherein Gum Tragacanth hath been soaked. You may use this for Sope, when you wash your hands, for they scowre them and make them white.

Magick Dew

For a beautiful Face, wash daily in Dew upon which the Sun hath not shone. Collect Dew before dawn by dragging a new sheet over the grass and wringing it out into a bucket. Keep it close stopped in an earthern Jar that the Sun's Rays reach it not and destroy its virtue.

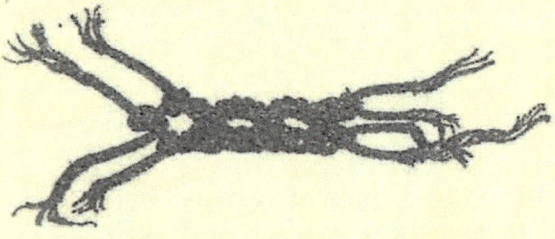

With mice, fill an earthern pip-kin. Stop the mouth with a lump of clay and bury it beside a fire but so as the fire be not too great and reach it not. So be it left for a year and after that time take out whatsoever may be found therein, but it is urgent that he who takes it have a glove on his hand, lest at his finger ends the hair shall sprout.

It says little for the sense of humour of the occult world that such obvious leg-pulls as the above "cure for baldness" have been gravely preserved over the centuries. Aimed at deflating the male vanity of some thinly thatched bumpkin, it continues to fool the humourless.

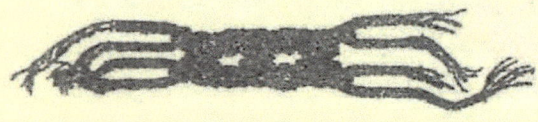

Rose Sachet

ake a pound of dried pink Rose Buds and crush them in a mortar. Add half a pound of Yellow Sandalwood Raspings and a quarter of an ounce of Otto of Rose and stir the mixture well. Make pretty silk sachets and put half an ounce of the fragrant compound in each. This sachet is under the ruling of the gentle Venus.

Heliotrope Sachet

To two pounds of Orris Root Powder, add one pound of dried Pink Roses, half a pound of grated Tonka Beans and a quarter pound of chopped Vanilla Pods. Add a quarter ounce of Musk and ten drops of Otto of Almonds and form into sachets. This mixture comes under the dominion of the Sun.

L'AMOVREVX

Sweet Perfume

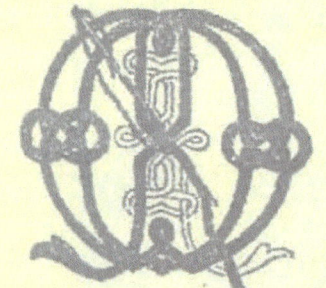 ost lovely and delicate of all the ancient Pagan Perfumes was an aromatic Sweet Almond Oil. It was made by saturating squares of cotton cloth in Sweet Almond Oil and sandwiching freshly picked flowers between them - a layer of blossoms and a square of oil-soaked cloth in alternate layers until a good pile was raised. Each day the flowers were discarded and fresh ones put in their place until the oil was impregnated with perfume. The cloths were then wrung out and the oil filtered and bottled. It was used to perfume the body after bathing.

Lavender Sachet

ust as a simple Rose Sachet consists of much more than Rose Petals, a real old-fashioned Lavender Sachet contains many things in addition to Lavender. Here is a typical 17th. century Lavender Sachet recipe:-

To an ounce of Lavender Flowers add one dram of Lavender Oil, a dram of Oil of Bergamot and a dram of Oil of Neroli. Mix this with a quarter of an ounce each of Dried Mint, Dried Thyme, Carraway Seeds, Ground Cloves and Benzoin. When sewn into sachets and placed amongst clothing, this mixture will continue to impart its rich perfume for many months.

A Lavender Suffumigation

Lavender is ruled by Mercury who governs, amongst other things, the art of healing. Small wonder then that Lavender Incense was used to freshen the sick room.

It is quite simply made by immersing loosely tied bundles of Lavender stalks in a saturated solution of Saltpetre for ten days. When thoroughly dried, they are used one at a time like Joss Sticks. So simple!

To Mayke A Speciall Sweet Water
To Perfume Clothing

All these thynges put into a glasse with a quart of Damaske Rose Water. A handfulle of Lavender Flowers, two ounces of Orris, a drachm of Muske, the weight of fourpence of Ambergreese, as much Civet and five drops of Oil of Cloves. Stop thys close and set it in the Sunne for a fortnight. Put a spoonfulle of the perfume in a basin of Spring Water to perfume thy clothes in the folding of them being washed.

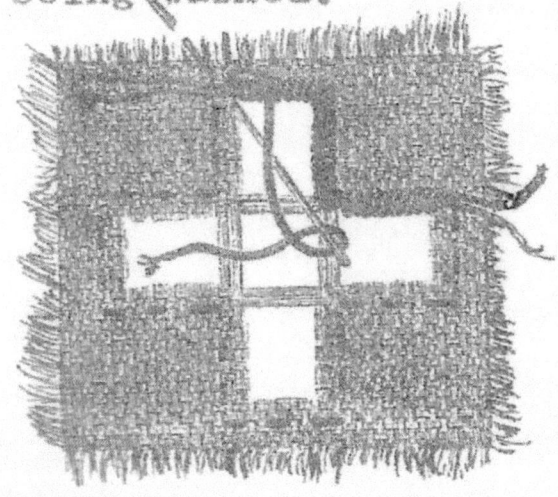

Love Smoke

ake one and a half pounds of finest seirced Willow Charcoal, four ounces of Labdanum, three drachms of Storax, two of Benjamin and one of Cedarwood. Mix the Storax, Benjamin, and Labdanum in a heated Mortar. Add the Charcoal and Cedarwood powdered. Put unto these, half an ounce of Liquid Storax, then dissolve Gum Acacia in Rosewater and add by degrees into the mortar to form an unguent.

Mould the substance into the shapes of little birds and animals and paint them over with Musk or Ambergris dissolved in Grape Spirit, and put them to dry in the shade.

When you do burn them in a censer or on a plate you will receive a most sweet fume like to fill the heart of any man with Love. And when you burn this perfume look boldly in the eyes of thy love and contrive that thy hand shall touch his or that thy hair shall brush his cheek, and it were a miracle if he love you not.

Rhyme & Reason

eclarations of intent, often in rhyme, are an essential part of many real traditional spells.

These spoken charms have now degenerated into superstition. Originally however they were regarded as the link between ideas and their manifestation as facts in the world of physical reality. The purpose of the spoken charm is to transform a wish or aim from a vague yearning into a definite declaration of the intention of bringing it into physical realisation. Without this dynamic determination to follow up the charm with immediate and positive creative action, the words become mere mumbo-jumbo without reason. When a direct attempt to fulfil the aim of the spell was impracticable, the action that followed or accompanied the oral declaration of intent had to be symbolic. This accounts for some of the quaint rituals associated with folk spells.

Throughout life it is vitally necessary to transform thought into physical reality by means of decisive action. This is a fact denied by a great many of those occultists who advocate meditation and "Spiritual exercises". Man, being an inherently idle animal, is only too willing to accept a doctrine of physical immobility, particularly if it holds the promise of "powers" too great to be entrusted to ordinary mortals.

True Magick faces the fact that we live in a real world where it is sometimes more effective to use a pick and shovel than to sit contemplating one's navel! There are more ways of killing a cat than drowning it in cream and there are numberless methods for achieving a magickal result. The important factor is that, regardless of method or technique, the end product must be real by the standards of the world in which we live.

A Tissane To Increase Milk

Infuse an ounce of Goat's Rue in a pint of spring water and allow it to cool. Add a little honey and it will take away the bitterness. A small cupful taken twice daily will help the flow of milk in a nurse and if beer also be drunk, so much the better.

(Goat's Rue has always had a reputation as a galactagogue and is the active ingredient in a widely advertised bust developer!)

Whooping Cough

To cure the chincough, take some housemice, flaw them and dry them in an oven; then make them into fine powder and let the party take as much of the powder as will lye on a broad shillinge, in beer or possett, first in the morning and last at night.

(Eliz. Freke 1671).

A Charm Against A Witch-Wound

Loud   were   they, lo!   loud
When   over   the   lew   they   rode.
They   were   of   stout mood.
When   over   the   lew   they   rode.
Shield   thee   now;   thou mayest save this nithing.
Out little spear; if herein it be.
He stood under the linden   broad,
Under   a   light   shield,
Where   the   mighty   witch   wives
Their main strength proved.
And   yelling   they   sent darts.
I   again will   send   them another
Flying feathered bolt from the front against them.
Out little spear; if herein it be.
Sat the smith; he sledged a sword.
Little   iron, wound   sharp,
Out little spear; if herein it be.

Six smiths sat,
Slaughter spears they wrought.
Out spear, not, in spear.
If herein there be, of iron a bit,
A witches work,
It shall melt.
If thou wert on fell shotten,
Or wert on flesh shotten,
Never let thy life be a teazed.
If it were an aesir shot,
Or if it were an elfin shot,
Or if it were a witches shot,
Now will I help thee.
Here's this to boot of aesir shot,
Here's this to boot of elfin shot,
Here's this to boot of witches shot,
I will help thee.
Fled Thor to the mountain.
Hallows he had two.
May the Lord help thee!"

Wart Cures

Of many hundreds of wart charms, here are but a few:-

Find a pebble for each wart, touching each wart with a different pebble. Put the pebbles in a red flannel bag. Go for a walk and throw the bag over your left shoulder without looking back. An uncharitable charm as it is said that the person who picks up the bag will get the warts!

Dandelion juice is said to banish warts if applied when the Moon is waning.

If warts are rubbed with a piece of bacon fat which is then concealed in a slit made in the bark of an Elder Tree, it is thought that they will be cured.

Another method is to cut a notch in a growing Elder branch for each wart. As the notches heal, the warts are said to disappear.

The Mountain Ash has a reputation as a wart curer. Push a pin for each wart into the bark of the tree, saying as you do so:-
"ROWAN TREE, ROWAN TREE,
PRAY BUY THESE WARTS OF ME."

The simplest wart spell is to rub each wart with the fluffy inside of a broad bean shell and then to bury the shells where they will not be disturbed.

Charm For A Sprain

To be recited whilst stroking the limb.

"PHOL AND WODEN
RODE TO THE WOOD
WHERE BALDUR'S FOAL
WRENCHED ITS FOOT.
THEN WODEN CHARMED
AS HE WELL KNEW HOW;
AS FOR BONE-WRENCH
SO FOR BLOOD-WRENCH;
BONE TO BONE,
BLOOD TO BLOOD,
LIMB TO LIMB,
AS IF THEY WERE GLUED!"

An Ague Charm

This charm was called up the chimney by the eldest female of the family.

"TREMBLE AND GO!
FIRST DAY
SHIVER AND BURN:
TREMBLE AND QUAKE!
SECOND DAY
SHIVER AND LEARN:
TREMBLE AND DIE!
THIRD DAY
NEVER RETURN!"

Another Ague Charm

ave three horse shoes nailed to the foot of the bed, points upwards. Take a hammer in the left hand and strike each shoe in turn, saying:-

"FATHER,   SON   AND   HOLY   GHOST,
NAIL   THE   DEVIL   TO   THE   POST.
THRICE   I   SMITE   WITH   HOLY   CROCK,
WITH   THIS HAMMER   THRICE DO   KNOCK.
ONE   FOR   GOD!
ONE   FOR   WOD!
AND ONE FOR LOK!

A Charm Against Burns

Lay   your   hand   on   the   spot   and
say   in   a   clear   voice:-

"HERE   COME   I
TO   CURE A BURN'D SORE.
IF   THE   DEAD   KNEW
WHAT THE LIVING ENDURE;
THE   BURN'D   SORE
WOULD   BURN   NO   MORE!"

and   then   blow   on   the   place
three   times.

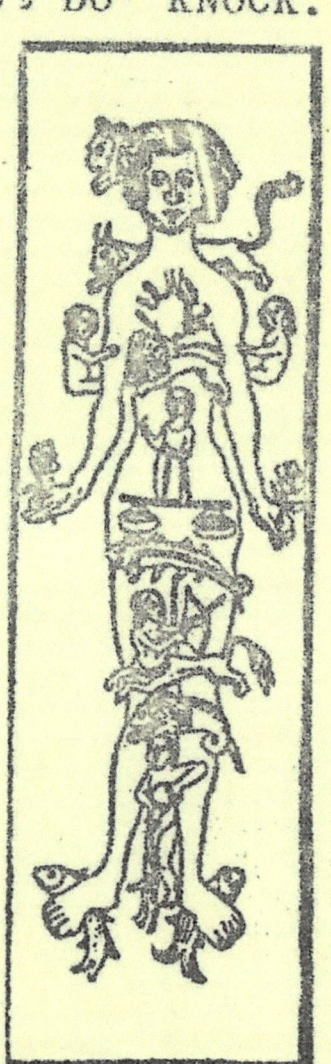

Some Curious Rural Beliefs

FOR HEADACHES.

Sew the cast skin of a Viper in the lining of your hat.

FOR RHEUMATISM.

Join together a piece of brass, zinc and copper and carry it in your pocket.

FOR NEURALGIA.

Powdered Brimstone should be put in the shoe on the side opposite to the pain.

FOR SLEEPLESSNESS.

When you go to bed have the tooth of a Fox under your pillow.

FOR LUMBAGO.

A mixture of Oil of Lavender, Oil of Guaiacwood , and Oil of Juniper. Take a single drop on a lump of sugar before retiring.

Betony Salve

Take a good handful of each of the following herbs: Balm, Sage, Southernwood, Rosemary, Wood Betony, Chamomile, Lavender, Feverfew, Red Rosebuds and Wormwood. Strip all from the stalks and chop the leaves fine and boil them in one and a quarter pounds of fresh Lard in the oven for two or three hours. Strain by squeezing through a linen cloth and then store in small earthenware jars.

For a bruise, rub gently with the salve. For an inward bruise take a piece the size of a nut in hot beer at bed-time.

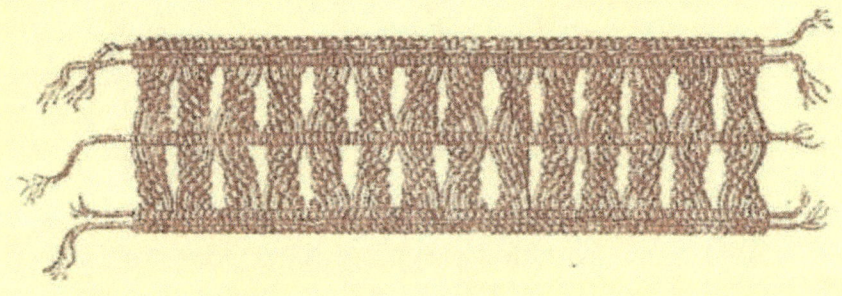

Nettle Stings

To cure a nettle sting, rub the part with a docken leaf saying:-

"NETTLE OUT, DOCK IN.
DOCK REMOVE NETTLE STING."

The Healing Charm
Of Agnes Sampson

ALL KINDS OF ILLS THAT EVER MAY BE,

IN CHRIST'S NAME, I CONJURE YE.

I CONJURE YE, BOTH MORE AND LESS

WITH ALL THE VIRTUES OF THE MESSE

AND RIGHT SO, BY THE NAILS SO,

THAT NAILED JESUS, AND NO MORE:

AND RIGHT SO, BY THE SAME BLOOD

THAT REEKED OVER THE RUTHFUL ROOD;

FORTH OF THE FLESH AND OF THE BONE,

AND IN THE EARTH AND IN THE STONE,

I CONJURE THEE, IN GOD'S NAME!

Four Thieves Vinegar

undreds of years ago, before disinfectants were thought of, people made use of aromatic vinegars which were added to washing water or carried as an inhalant in a perforated container called a vinaigrette. Most famous of all toilet vinegars was a French recipe called "Vinaigre des Quatre Voleurs" or "Four Thieves Vinegar."

The legend tells of four thieves who were sentenced to death for robbing plague victims during the Plague of Paris. The authorities, curious to know how the villains avoided catching the dreaded Bubonic Plague, offered a pardon in return for their secret. The thieves revealed that, before setting out on their horrible mission, each hung round his neck a sponge soaked in a special vinegar. Here is the formula which they disclosed!

"VINAIGRE DES QUATRE VOLEURS"

INTO FOUR PINTS OF WHITE WINE VINEGAR PUT THREE QUARTERS OF AN OUNCE OF EACH OF THE FOLLOWING HERBS; WORMWOOD, ROSEMARY, SAGE, MINT AND RUE. ADD AN OUNCE OF LAVENDER FLOWERS AND ONE DRACHM EACH OF GARLIC, CALAMUS, CINNAMON, CLOVES AND NUTMEG.

ALLOW THE MIXTURE TO DIGEST AT SUMMER HEAT IN A CLOSED GLASS VESSEL FOR FOURTEEN DAYS. EXPRESS AND FILTER AND THEN ADD HALF AN OUNCE OF CAMPHOR OR OIL OF CAMPHOR DISSOLVED IN AN OUNCE OF SPIRITS OF WINE.

To Break A Spell

f you think you have been bewitched, buy an iron nail and a new hammer without haggling. Go alone to a crossroads at midnight and when the clock begins to strike turn round three times sunwise and hammer the nail into the ground up to the head.

Walk away backwards before the clock finishes striking. At the last stroke of the hour turn and go home, throwing the hammer away over your left shoulder and speaking no word until you have crossed your own threshold.

The Mandragore

Mandrake is not a specific plant but simply a basic universal concept. That is why the primitive idea of a semi-human plant, although common to every race, is associated with so many different plants.

In China, it is the rare Ginseng that is reputed to grow in human form. German peasants regarded the Alraun - the carved root of the Rowan tree - as the real Mandragore. Biblical literature refers to the poisonous "Atropa Mandragora" as being the true Mandrake. English Mandrake is "Bryonia Dioica" whose fleshy root can grow to a massive size and whose flowers indicate by their form the gender of the root.

All these plants have one thing in common. Each is capable of being transformed by means of a ritual involving carving, transplanting and special cultivation, into a Mandragore.

Plant or Woman? A Dream out of the Universal Unconscious.
THE ALRAUN MAIDEN.

he real secret of the Mandragore lies in the mystical form of preparation that changes it from a plant into a symbol of the link between one form of life and another. Although

Bryonia Dioica

the controversy over which plant was the true Mandrake reached such proportions that people were hanged for selling one rather than another, the important fact was being overlooked. The only esoteric virtue of the Mandragore lay in the fact that the owner had obtained and prepared it with his own hands. The act of preparation was a potent piece of mind manipulation and the finished Mandragore was treated with awe and respect, primarily because it represented a personified fragment of its creator's own consciousness.

Those who continue to wrangle over whether the one true Mandrake happens to be "Panax Ginseng" or "Atropa Mandragora", have fallen into the trap of all intellectuals in that they are confusing the symbol with the fact. Botanically, there are great differences between the many versions of the universal "man-root". Mystically they are all identical.

Panax Ginseng

Butterfly Magick

prinkle bushes and shrubs with sugar-water to which a few drops of best Oil of Lavender have been added.

If the day is warm and sunny, it will not be very long before your garden is filled with the colourful spectacle of a myriad gay butterflies attracted to the tempting mixture.

To Catch Fish

Moisten the bait with Rhodium Oil, Cedarwood Oil and Juniper Oil blended in equal parts.

Another way to obtain fish is to make cakes of flour, water and Valerian Root and throw these in the water. Fish that eat of them will become intoxicated and float to the surface where they may be taken in the hand.

Rose Petal Jam

 oak a pound of fresh red rose petals in a quart of water for thirty minutes, covering the basin with a damp cloth. Pour off the water and keep it. Place the petals and one third of the saved water, together with seven pounds of finest white sugar, in a preserve pan and leave covered for a day and a night. Now add half of the remaining water and boil for about ten minutes. Add the rest of the water, a little at a time and boil until the mixture is of a creamy thickness. Add the juice of a large lemon. Stir well and pot in small jars for special occasions.

Bee Wine

To an ounce of yeast, add two pints of lukewarm water and a level tablespoonful of sugar. Use a sweet jar with a bladder tied over the neck to hold the mixture. Keep at a summer temperature and feed the "bees" with a teaspoonful of sugar daily to keep them working, being careful to replace the bladder each time. After ten days or more, the wine may be poured off and bottled for drinking in six weeks. Bee Wine may be flavoured with lemon or other fruit juice.

Three Thousand Years ago
my incenses perfumed the
Temples of Egypt

Witch's Delight

A WINE RECIPE FROM THE PENDLE HILL DISTRICT

 oil two pounds of sugar and one pound of chopped raisins in a gallon of spring or rain water for one and a half hours. Add a quarter pound of honey to the liquid. Stir till dissolved and pour the lot over Mistletoe Herb, Motherwort, Valerian Root and Wood Betony; of each one and a half ounces.

When the brew has cooled to blood heat add an ounce of fresh yeast and let the wine ferment for six weeks in a covered vessel. Strain and bottle and keep for three months.

You don't have to be a witch to enjoy this wine when it is properly made.

Some Traditional Suffumigations

One of the appropriate incenses burned at the right planetary hour was thought to aid many kinds of undertaking. The ingredients were mixed and then sprinkled on glowing charcoal.

To bless and purify a newly entered abode, the incense used was a mixture of Camphor, Myrtle and Nutmeg.

When honours were being sought, an incense composed of Benjamin, Pepperwort and Cedar might help things along.

For new ventures of all kinds, success was assured by the helpful fragrance of Red Storax, Sandalwood and Nutmeg.

For enduring Love and lasting Friendship, the suffumigation was Saffron and Pepperwort.

Students seeking academic success were advised to burn Mastic and Cinnamon to aid their studies.

Those seeking to banish enemies burned the overpowering combination of Cayenne Pepper and Guiacwood.

For inducing prophetic dreams, the favourite choice of incense was Coriander Seeds and Sandalwood.

Gamblers burned Mastic and Frankincense for luck at games of chance.

An incense of Galbanum and Saffron was believed to strengthen the personality and attract the opposite sex.

When financial gains were sought, the speculator might resort to the use of a mixture of Pepperwort, Saffron and Nutmeg.

To cleanse a room after sickness, the fumes of White Resin, Salt, Sulphur and Myrrh were thought to be effective

47

nd Nature, the old nurse, took
The child upon her knee.
Saying "Here is a story-book
Thy Father has written for thee."
"Come wander with me," she said,
"Into regions yet untrod,
And read what is still unread
In the Manuscript of God."

Longfellow .

THE END

48

Designed, written, made,
printed and published

by

Margaret Bruce

at

The Angèl Press, 166 Yarm Road,
DARLINGTON. Co. Durham, England.

The Angel Press, 166 Yarm Road
DARLINGTON, Co. Durham

Printed in Dunstable, United Kingdom